Poem of Poems
Short Poetry

Milford John-Williams Sr.

Poem of Poems: Short Poetry
This book is written to provide information and motivation to readers. Its purpose is not to render any type of psychological, legal, or professional advice of any kind. The content is the sole opinion and expression of the author, and not necessarily that of the publisher.

Copyright © 2020 by Milford John-Williams Sr.

All rights reserved. No part of this book may be reproduced, transmitted, or distributed in any form by any means, including, but not limited to, recording, photocopying, or taking screenshots of parts of the book, without prior written permission from the author or the publisher. Brief quotations for noncommercial purposes, such as book reviews, permitted by Fair Use of the U.S. Copyright Law, are allowed without written permissions, as long as such quotations do not cause damage to the book's commercial value. For permissions, write to the publisher, whose address is stated below.

ISBN 978-1-953150-12-7 (Paperback)
ISBN 978-1-953150-13-4 (Digital)

Lettra Press books may be ordered through booksellers or by contacting:

Lettra Press LLC
30 N Gould St. Suite 4753
Sheridan, WY 82801, USA
1 307-200-3414 | info@lettrapress.com
www.lettrapress.com

Introduction

Poetry is a way of expressing emotional feelings of joy or sadness through dialogue. In this book the dialogue of self aperture is been conveyed in the simplest form of text that everyone who read the short poetry in this book will understand, and may somehow see themselves as caption in some of the poetry. If you do, feel free to sink yourself into it and read it loud for fun.

For example "The Magnificent Dreamers" is a true experience while working with special needs children, you can always see the joy and appreciation the smiles in their faces, but cannot fully expressed themselves.

"A Cradle in the Dark" you always hear about people give birth to a child and just left them somewhere, if they are Lucky to be found by someone.

Poetry is also a creative way of visualizing character and events through dramatization. Our lives are poetic in many ways when we recognize our mortal existence in this world.

Acknowledgement

This is my vision of writing a poetry book. While I made an effort to write this book, it include many important images in my head and daily experience of event in my surroundings. One could write volume of books or poetry, but the key is to make readers develop an understanding of the structure of the book or poem.

This book could not have been completed without the input and encouragement of some very important and special people.

To Rebecca Kubiak, a Language Arts Teacher at Mountain View High School, Stafford Virginia; whose class the Idea of writing poetry started, when I was in her classroom with a special student of mine; Frank Adair (Kyle). She was teaching the contrast of poetry and prose, and how the students should learn to develop critical thinking skills. It was in her classroom I wrote my first poem. In completion of the poem I showed it to her, her approval was very positive which gave me the confidence on my writing skills.

To Mrs. Kreseau, a Language Teacher in creative writing, was the first to edit my poems and inspired me to believe that I can publish my writing.

To Mr. Jon Day a world History Teacher, whose history class. The Poetry of the "Gold God and Glory" following his teaching on exploration.

To Kyle Adair who always inspired me to write something every time I said I have finish writing one poem.

To the Mountain View High School Publication "The Viewpoint" was the first to publish one of my poem "The Magnificent Dreamers" written especially for the teachers and paraprofessionals of the MD and Autism rooms at Mountain View High School.

To Mrs. Melissa McClellan, who gave me the opportunity to be part of the Mountain View High School family, where it all started.

Early in the morning

As I tossed and turn in my bed.
I opened my eyes, glanced at my window
With a ray of reflection from a street light.
It was dark early in the morning.

I got up from my bed as I stretched
walked to the window paced back and forth
the shiny floor as she squirts
It is dark early in the morning.

I sat for a while and watched the Television.
The morning news was on the air
I turned my head look to the window again
It is dark early in the morning.

It's going to be a beautiful day
Said the weatherman, arise and shine
minutes past, I walked towards the window
It's still dark early in the morning.

The hope for sunrise or brighter morning
Seemed longer and longer behind a shadow
anything more than darkness is long for.
Yes it's still dark early in the morning.

The beginning of the day dragged
while the body was willing to thrive
as the sound of the birds whispered
Yes it's still dark early in the morning.

Be Merry and Happy

In the morning when you wake up
You arise for your daily chores
You experience entering a new day
Be Merry and Happy.

As your shower flows on you
You feel awakened to your call
for it is the beginning of a new day
Be Merry and Happy.

Time passes as you prepare for work
time passes as you leave your home
time passes as you go along
Be Merry and Happy.

For this day will be tomorrow
make use of the moment and time
cherishing the things you will not borrow
Be Merry and Happy.

The day may not be that of your choice
For the challenges of life is not certain
relinquish the day for what it is
Be Merry and be Happy.

The walls we face

Why stay behind the walls we face
When you can break through cracks
With an opening to fill with grace
Courage and determination pursue

Take a chance with no fear
Go forward head on don't look back
For nothing attempt, nothing done
If try once, try twice and try again

Success doesn't come without trying
Sometimes we fail because we scare
Sometimes we fail because we don't try
Sometimes we fail because we're not sure

We are ourselves, but no one else
Our future is in our hands
Our success is in our hands
Our failure is in our hands
Don't limit yourself to what you can do
I can't do it is no excuse
Sitting back is no excuse
And being lazy is not that cute

The Person you should

You are what you are, to be that
Be better than the person you were yesterday
Never regrets anything that defines you
You are the person you should

Sun may rise clouds will flow
Light and darkness may come and go
The day may move slowly
You are the person you should

When time seem to be assuring
But it's just much to be adoring
Disappointment may trigger hanger
You are the person you should

Time constraint your involvement
As you ascend to the pinnacle of trust
To capture the preference of tranquility
You are the person you should

Fearlessness, bigotry and hopelessness
Will conceal you to wonder if and why
No matter what, you prevail sincerely
You are the person you should

That's The Way We Were

In early years you wonder around daily
With your siblings, with your friends
Thinking of nothing but fun and games
Because that's the way we were

There is always a lesson to learn
From your family friends and neighbors
The future might be bright but who cares
Because that's the way we were

School days are the best, not the happiest
Growing up and maturity linger our hearts
As we strive to make it through the years
Because that's the way we were

Walking through the halls we share
Was the path to bring us closer together
We were always loud and furious
Because that's the way we were

Summer was always fun and shorter
Driving in the blast of open air space
With an excitement of exploration
Because that's the way we were

As you like it

When you do it for yourself
There never a question of choice
You can be right, you can be wrong
It's all about how you like it

It can be long, it can be short
It can be high, it can be low
It can be wide, it can be small
It's all about how you like it

Do it fast, with no time to bare
Do it slow with all time to dare
Do it at your time with no fare
It's all about how you like it

You know how you want it to be
You know how to cut it and dice it
You know how to fold it or spread it
It's all about how you like it
You can share all of it with others
You can show all of it to others
You can live life in your own way
It's all about how you like it.

The Magnificent dreamers

We can see the world differently
For our perspective are unimaginable
We see all the things you see
But the reflection is in our hearts
Because we are the magnificent Dreamers

The things you touches everyday
We feel deeply in our hearts
The sounds you hear everyday
We hear too, but stay in our minds
Because we are the magnificent Dreamers

The words you say to us we stored
The good things you do for us shows
As we recognized diligently with a smile
Which demonstrate our love for you
Because we are the magnificent Dreamers

The food you give us each day
The nourishment shows in our body
We may not say a word or two
But we know you are there
Because we are the magnificent Dreamers

We are not able to thank you with our voices
Your appreciation is felt in our hearts
We reach out with our hands to cheer you up
For you are the ones that touches our lives
Because we are the magnificent dreamers

Let bygones be bygones

When we feel hurt by someone
It's sometimes had to understand
If you placed yourself in their shoes
You will see, feel and think differently
Because humans are not perfect

Circumstances may dictate our decisions
Which may linger our behavior perfect or imperfect
If we stop to think wisely and clearly
Our patience will serve us dearly
Don't be judge mental to others

Forget about unpleasant things in the past
What's done is done, don't worry about it
Holding on to the past, destroyed the present
The present will always be bright
When you shed the light to forgive

Remember what goes around comes around
You might be on this side today
Tomorrow you'll be on the other side
Time and tide waits for no one
Don't let the past holds you back

The Escalator

As I walked through the double doors
A twin tower of elevated steps are there
A structure of metals and rubber rails
One goes up and one goes down

People goes up and down all day long
Kids runs up and down the stairs
It's look like a fun and jolly ride
When you know how to get on it

When crowded is not that fun
Hustling and buffing through the stairs
Luggage fell off, come tumbling down
Crashed on the floor and make a mess

No one stop to help with care
People walked bye, they do not care
Looked at the floor like nothing is there
Helpfulness is no where to be found

The escalator squill quietly to the top
The escalator squill quietly to the ground
Going up and down all day long
For those who don't want to stair.

Pain pain go away

Pain pain where are you, go away
Don't come back another day
I want to talk and laugh with gesture
I want to walk and run with pleasure

Your presence will destroy my pasture
I want to eat and taste all flavor
I want to drink and enjoy the vigor
I want to touch and feel the texture

I want to jump and bounce around
Your presence will destroy my pasture
I want to see the world and it's view
I want to relax and enjoy the view

I want to bend without you there
I want to sleep without you in my bed
Your presence will destroy my pasture
I don't want your pinching and sensation

I don't want your throbbing and pulsation
You hurt and I don't feel comfortable
Your sever discomfort cause me agony
Your presence will destroy my pasture

I need my head to think for my being
I need my heart to motion circulation
I need my stomach for body consumption
I need myself to be myself without you
For your presence will destroy my pasture

Brighter Vision seems afar

When you thirst for yonder tomorrow
You take a step forward in space
But you find yourself two steps back
You think you are going up wards
You find yourself down looking up

Trying harder doesn't seem to matter
As you stroll down the path of courage
You can see the shining light ahead
The further you go so is the light
Wondering when time will stand still

Ho, How quickly time flies bye
Walking through the fields of dream
Wishing that time will come to light
When all the desires of distance promises
Will fulfill all your future accomplishment

Brighter vision seems so far away
When all I've done is to see the light
Keep following the light till you reach it
Keep climbing till you make it to the top
The light will be there, when you get there

Gold, God And Glory

Historians reasons for world exploration
Motivates to generate overseas expansion
European conquest of countries to rise
Acquiring and selling resources of lands
Merchants gained influence to reign
All for Gold, God and Glory.

Gold truly drove the Europeans to explore
World wealth makes their kingdom stronger
They desired richness for personal wealth
Christopher Columbus Indigenous trader
Brought Spain a great profit and wealth
All for Gold, God and Glory.

God and religion in colonial conquered land
European spread Christianity to convert
Spread the Gospel to the rest of the world
Religion became enslaving exploitation
Allowed kingdom to participate in slave trade
All for Gold, God and Glory.

Glory, was a relative new idea in Europe
Came out of the Renaissance ideal of humanism
Kings and Queens wanted Glory for their kingdom
New mind sets and technology gained fame
Explorers seek personal Glory in the new world
All for Gold, God and Glory.

Magellan, searched for passage to the pacific
Hudson, found the northwest passage to Asia
Amerigo Vespucci mapped and name New land
Pizzaro, wanted to spread Catholicism in the Americas
Gold, God, and Glory known as three G's
Together fostered the golden age of Exploration.

A Cradle in the Dark

I was there like I wasn't there at all
No one noticed the cradle in the dark
My presence is absent in sight
Left in a building steps in the dark
As time whispers through the air

The sense of sound became meaningful
When I was found by a Goddess of soul
I was nurtured with careening and love
Family, trust, comforting and joy
My life was filled with kindness

My existence became meaningful
The world is now a better place for me
While in the twilight of the horizon
I long for a question of modem
That I knew the answer is far fetched

But I always wonder, Why me ? Why.
For the worst, sometimes brings out the best.
There is a reason for any purpose on earth
Now I see the world and the world sees me
I am part of the people in the world.

Today I can see myself, for who I am
My life is a symbol of a successful tales
A pillow of a cradle in the dark
For from the day you're burned
Your path of lives journey is destined

Sunrise and Sunset

As the early clouds glows in the east
The twill of light reflects at a distance
Slowly the shadow of darkness disappears
Rising from the burst of clouds is the sun
Oh, what a sight of natural wonder

The beauty of dawn light covers the clouds
The colors of the horizon are so glorious
Darkness became light in the sphere
Brighter sunshine through out the day
The morning became at the peak of the sun

The sun centers the sky at noon
As our shadows following our steps
Building and trees cast shadows of shades
People and animals moves shadows of rays
The brightness of sunshine reflect our shadows

East, west, north and south, our shadows moves
Down, Down, the sun set in the west
Darkness returned, and the day is gone
For the day is over as sun sets in the west
No more shades nor shadow of movement.

A long way from home

A long was, away from home
Traveling a journey so far and wide
Miles and miles of open land and sea
Where all creatures run wild and free

The highways and byways trail the land
As we drove through from place to place
Exploring the beauty of the open space
The atmosphere is for all to share

Sailing through the wide blue sea
Gusting winds blows through the air
Stopping to see and feel the air
Birds and Animals glazed along with pride

As destination gets closer ahead
Longer the distance away from home
Cruising along the meadows and valleys
To reach the point of distance halt

Home sweet home, so far away
The dwelling we love with family and friends
We shall return when the journey is over
We are a long way away from home.

The Rock of Ages

I am the rock, shiny and bright
I am the rock, girls best friend
I am the rock, measured in carats
I am the rock, polished for value
I am the rock, you love to wear
I am the rock, the rock of ages.

I am the rock, of all the rocks
I am the rock, you look for everywhere
I am the rock, that cuts with style
I am the rock, no one will compare
I am the rock, that brings you love
I am the rock, the rock of ages

I am the rock, the rock that cuts glass
I am the rock, I am smooth on fingers
I am the rock, attractive to the eyes
I am the rock, I am very expensive
I am the rock, you buy with a smile
I am the rock, the rock of ages

I am the rock, no matter the size
I am the rock, you carry everywhere
I am the rock, that makes you look good
I am the rock, that makes people jealous
I am the rock, that starts with the letter D
I am the rock, can you tell what am I.

Never say Never

Never say Never, for life is unpredictable
You never know what the future holds
For any day, is just another day
A day with new trials and tribulations

Never say never before assumptions
If there is anything you can do today
Do it today and don't wait for the morrow
Today is now, for you know the present

Never say never, shot doors of opportunity
The future might be good or bad
Make use of the moment and time
Don't waste precious opportunities

Never say never, limit your expectations
Where success or failure relinquish
The choices you make depends on it
Embraced whatever it may be

Never say never, stabilize you transgressions
Try to reach for the challenges ahead
When adversity constrained your effort
You will never regret the result of trying

Never say never, when you can say I will
Believe in yourself and do it for yourself
The sky is the limit, how far can you reach
You will never regret, because you try.

Alone in the Moonlight

There is a place somewhere away so bright
A place with no buildings and no light
A place so quiet in the dark, but peaceful
A place where you feel the freshness in the air
As I found myself alone in the moonlight

It was night time in a lonely highway through
It was bright even though it was dark
I looked up in the sky is this bowl of light
It's shines so bright with a twinkly rays
As I found myself alone in the moonlight

I looked up again as the sky capture my eyes
With shooting stars, around the ray of light
Oh what a sight, so beautiful and glorious
The feeling of array you can't feel anywhere
As I found myself alone in the moonlight

When darkness falls upon the face of the earth
We experience the shadow of the universe
When darkness covers the clouds as they flows
We are overwhelmed with the light of dawn
As I found myself alone in the moonlight

When the darkness fades away in the morning
Sunlight returns and the beginning of a new day
I can see the light of the day is not that of night
The florescent of the moon captivate the night
That mystify my being alone in the moonlight

Fly like an eagle and be free

Be free as you fly over the universal trail
The world is an open sphere for all
Explore the beauty of sunrise and sunset
Glide your wings as your body flows
Fly like an eagle and be free

Spread your wings, so far and wide, as you can
Upward and downward, as fast as you can
Visions of captions some so near, some so far
Earth creation is the beauty of them all
Fly like an eagle and be free.

Beautiful flowers and greens mask the earth
Shoreline and valleys, separates land masses
Sounds of life echoes through out
See it all and feel it all, from above and bellow
Fly like an Eagle and be free.

The sky is closer, but yet so far away
Higher and higher I rise for the sky
Closer and closer I reach for the clouds
Open and closed clouds, floats in the air
Fly like an eagle and be free.

Fly alone, fly away, as fast as you can
Fly over the clouds, as fast as you can
Bounce over the clouds if you can
Float with the clouds if you can
Fly like an eagle and be free

Romance in the Sun

Somewhere beneath the sun is love
Romance seem to favor the motions
Away somewhere into the Atlantic paradise
The Ocean surface is clear and clean
Coral reefs are diverse under the water

Beaches and shorelines spread sea banks
As the sun shines, you feel love in the air
Couple hold hands with bikinis and shorts
Sipping margaritas, piñata colada and tequila
Enjoying the moment as time passes bye

How Romantic walking along the seashores
The wet sands and the sound of the waves
Surfers roaming the waters at wave length
The atmosphere transcends love and feelings
Making our emotions more memorable.

The shores echoes the sounds in the air
As we relaxes in the highland of paradise
We experience the twilight of life's adventure
Under the twilight raise of the blazing sun
Romance in the sun, what we thrived and feel

The cumulus clouds below the blue sky
Reflect the shinny blue sea ocean
The smell of freshness and purity in the air
Winds blowing from different directions off shores
Romance in the sun, what we thrive and feel

Then and Now

If I had known then, what I know now
What would my life be like yesterday and today
What will I be doing to make ends meet
What kind of decisions will I be making
What kind of friends will I associate with
Will it make me wiser and stronger

Will I be the same person who someone adores
Will I be living the way of life am living now
Will all things that flourished around me be there
Will the road to success be on my path
Will family life be something I long for
If I had known then, what I know now

Will my curiosity be overwhelming
Will my confidence be appalling
Will my accomplishment defines me
Will I be socially wild and crazy
Will I dedicate myself to a life time of service
If I had known then, what I know now

Will it be the key to my happiness
Will I be acknowledged by all my peers
Will my character be truly endure
Will it guarantees me a brighter future
What ever happened then and now
Makes you the person you are today

A Friend in need, a friend indeed

A friend is someone who reflects you
Someone who believes in your views
Someone who shares your values
Someone who relates to you
Someone who understands you
A friend in need, is a friend indeed

Someone who consider you as a partner
Someone who will stand up for you
Someone who will light you up
Someone who will be your right hand
Someone who is more than a friend
A friend is never known till you have need

Someone who sees your light and darkness
Someone who is willing to climb for you
Someone who is willing to fall for you
Someone who will never back down
Someone who support you at all cost
A friend in need is a friend in deed.

Someone who celebrate your happiness
Someone who courage your sadness
Someone who will go the distance with you
Someone who demonstrate Love and Fairness
Someone who is always there for you
A friend in need is a friend indeed.

Jesus Is Stripped Of His Garments

Why would anyone want to take Jesus 'clothes?.
As for me, I will be bound to him in spirit,
He is the way, the truth, and the light.
No one comes to the father, but through Him.
Why would you want to take Jesus 'clothes?.

Because of Him, I can see spiritual light.
Because of Him, I can praise the Lord.
Because of Him, I am free from sin
Because of Him, I am filled with joy.
Why would you want to take Jesus 'clothes?.

Some will say his clothes are made of silk
Some will say his clothes are made of velvet
Some will say his clothes are common materials
Some will say his clothes are priceless.
Why would you want to take Jesus 'clothes?.

I wonder if the soldiers could sense his grace,
That he is the beloved son of god
The mediator, and guidance for mankind
He knew what is; humiliation and pain
Why would you want to take Jesus 'clothes?.

Jesus, helped me to look past the outside.
He helped me, not to judge others by how they look.
He helped me, to find my self worth, and identity.
Love and guide me through all things.
Why would you want to take Jesus 'clothes?.

Oh Africa, Africa

Africa the second largest continent in the Globe,
With tumbling waves across the Atlantic Ocean.
Light sands covering the Oceanfront
Blue seas of coastline along it shores
Oh Africa, Africa.

Africa, Africa a huge plateau divided,
With the desert sands in the Sahara.
With the Gold-coast in the West
With wildlife Safari in the East.
Oh Africa, Africa.

Africa, known for the diversity of its people,
Countless ethnic groups inhabit its land,
Africa the Cradle of human Civilization
Africa the domain of European Colonial powers.
Oh Africa, Africa.

Africa, Africa land of natural resources,
Land of Diamond, Gold, Iron and Silver,
Land of Cocoa, Salt, and Sugar.
Land of Banana, Beans, peanuts and yams.
Oh Africa, Africa.

Africa, Africa unique in every unmeasurable ways,
Its people life cultures and religions,
It's season, rainy, sunny, hot and dry.
The Life of its people is always pleasant.
Oh Africa, Africa.

www.ingramcontent.com/pod-product-compliance
Lightning Source LLC
Chambersburg PA
CBHW071917070526
44583CB00016B/2029